**It's All My Fault!**

Written by Sharon Parsons
Illustrated by Bettina Guthridge

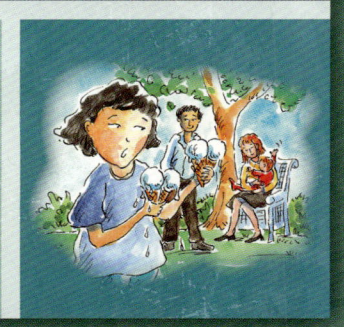

"Sometimes, when you try to help, nothing goes right. It's not always your fault. Sometimes, you just need some help."

Grusilda xxx

me

Mum

Dad

One morning, I spilt chocolate milk all over my shirt and pants.

"Whoops!" said Mum.

"It's all my fault," I said. "Sorry, Mum."

I wanted to help, so I went to the laundry.
I put my shirt and pants in the washing machine with some laundry powder. Then I added some other white clothes, too.

Then I turned on the washing machine.

But when the washing machine had washed my clothes, I got a shock. Some red colour had come out of my shirt and turned my white pants and all the white clothes pink!

"It's all my fault," I said. "Sorry, Mum."

"It's OK," said Mum.

Then I went to the kitchen to help Dad cook dinner for our family.

Dad told me to add a little bit of salt to the pan of potatoes.

"Yes Dad," I said, as I added the salt.

At dinner, all of us wanted to spit out the potatoes. They were too salty.

"Sorry," I said. "It's all my fault. I put too much salt on the potatoes."

Later, Mum told me to bring ice-creams for us to eat under the tree. But by the time I had put ice-cream in *every* cone, they started to melt!

"Sorry I took so long," I said. "Lick them quick!"

We licked our ice-creams quickly!

"We should have helped you," said Mum. "Now it's all *our* fault!"

"I think ice-creams **do** taste better when they are melting!" said Dad.

"Thank you," I smiled. "I feel better now."